History of Cub Libre!

Cuban History from Christopher Columbus to Fidel Castro

Carlos Fernando Alvarez

Table of Contents

Introduction 3

Chapter 1: Pre-Spanish and Spanish Occupation 5

Chapter 2: The Wars for Independence 9

Chapter 3: U.S. Occupation and the Platt Amendment 14

Chapter 4: Cuba's Reform Movements 17

Chapter 5: The Cuban Republic and Revolution 21

Chapter 6: The Castro Era 25

Chapter 7: Cuba in the Cold War Era 30

Chapter 8: Cuba-U.S. Relations and the Trade Embargo 34

Chapter 9: The History of Havana 40

Conclusion 43

Introduction

Cuba has a certain charm that may not be experienced anywhere else in the world. As a former Spanish colony, it shares numerous cultural traits with neighboring Caribbean, South American, and Central American countries. However, Cuba's history and political climate make the country a unique tourist attraction.

Cuba has a lot to offer each visitor. Tourists seeking privacy can enjoy a secluded vacation at an exclusive resort. Backpackers seeking to experience an authentic Caribbean culture may delight in the Havana neighborhoods. For those history aficionados, the colonial buildings and vintage cars would surely leave a mark.

The culture of Cuba is vibrant and varied, and its music – rumba, timba, and salsa, among other music styles – has become globally renowned. A visit to Cuba offers more than just a chance to bask in the Caribbean sun.

Before the 1950s, Cuba was a playground for European and American jetsetters. However, Cuba's alliance with the communist Soviet Union and its uneasy relationship with the United States curbed the influx of tourists for a number of years.

Since the 1990s, tourism experienced a resurgence and has become a vital part of the country's economy. Despite the country's political situation, the Cuban people maintain an openness and friendliness not usually found in other tourist destinations.

Tourists, especially those individuals interested in history, would be delighted to know more about how Cuba became the vibrant country it is today. The following chapters detail Cuba's history, from its Spanish colonial past, the country's involvement in various wars, important revolutionaries and leaders, the country's relationship with the United States, and other matters of historical significance.

Chapter 1: Pre-Spanish and Spanish Occupation

The first known residents of Cuba inhabited the island during the 4th millennium BCE. Levisa – Cuba's oldest known archaeological site – dates from around 3100 BCE. Other sites date from around 2000 BCE, most represented by western Cuba's Guayabo Blanco and Cayo Redondo cultures.

The Neolithic cultures used ground stone, shell ornaments, and tools, including the gladiolitos. The Guayabo Blanco and Cayo Redondo cultures followed a lifestyle of hunting, collecting wild plants, and fishing.

Before the arrival of Christopher Columbus, the Guanajatabey people, who had populated Cuba for centuries, were forced to vacate to the island's far west by the arrival of the Ciboney and Taino peoples, who had migrated from the South American mainland via the Caribbean island chain.

The Ciboney and Taino were part of the Arawak cultural group, who lived in South America before the Europeans' arrival. They first settled at Cuba's eastern portion before venturing out west. Bartolome de la Casas, a Spanish Dominican clergyman, estimated that the Taino people's population had reached 350,000 towards the end of the 15th century.

The Taino grew yucca, harvested the root crop, and baked it to make cassava bread. The Taino also grew tobacco and cotton, and ate sweet potatoes and maize.

In the History of the Indians, the Taino had "everything needed to live; they had many crops."

The Spanish Occupation

The arrival of Christopher Columbus in Cuba in 1492 heralded the start of Spanish occupation in the Americas. According to his journal, he had never seen anything so beautiful. Everything he saw was so lovely that his eyes could not tire of seeing such beauty; nor could he get tired of listening to the birds singing. According to him, there were thousands of tree species, with each tree bearing a unique fruit with a delicious flavor.

On the island, the Spanish prospected for gold. However, they did not know that the island's real value lay in its strategic location and rich soil. Cuba lies at the center of three major maritime routes: to the east (the Windward Passage), to the north (the Straits of Florida), and to the west (the Yucatan Channel) that enables both access to the Caribbean and the Gulf of Mexico.

At the intersection, Spain was the most vulnerable to foreign invasion. For two centuries, the country was a launching pad and home base for several important Spanish expeditions in the Americas. Cuba, which was dubbed the "Spanish fortress of the Caribbean," was touted by Spain as an important strategic colony.

The Ciboney and Taino people were the island's inhabitants when the Spaniards arrived, and they lived by farming, hunting, and fishing. Like the Puerto Rico Tainos, Cuba's Indian population was decimated by European diseases and hard labor. The Taino and

Ciboney cultivated tobacco and taught the Spaniards how to roll and smoke tobacco.

Spanish conquest in Cuba began nearly 20 years after Columbus arrived. The Cuban territory's control and conquest was handed over to Diego Velazquez, one of Hispaniola's richest landowners. The colonization process began in 1510. Warned of the Spanish activities on neighboring islands, Cuba's eastern aboriginals offered resistance against the invasion. Their leader, Hatuey, was caught and burned alive as an example.

In 1513, the village of Nuestra Señora de la Asunción de Baracoa was established. Seven other villages, with the intent of controlling the conquered lands, were created: Bayamo in 1513; Sancti Spiritus, Santisima Trinidad, and San Cristóbal de la Habana in 1514; Puerto Principe and Santiago de Cuba in 1515.

The economy of Cuba during the Spanish period was based on enslaving the native Indians, who were handed to the Spaniards via the 'encomienda' system, which was a non-transferable and revocable personal grant or concession. In the system, the colonizer must feed and clothe the natives, and teach them Christianity. The colonizer was then entitled to make the natives work for him. The encomienda system was a reason for the rapid decimation of the native Cuban population.

During the first years of colonization, the most significant economic activity was gold mining. Aside from Indians, the Spaniards also used Black slaves, who gradually integrated into the Cuban population. With the gold depleted, cattle soon turned into Cuba's main income source in the forms of leather and salted beef. At the same time, the Spaniards in Cuba started other forms of trade in the emerging Spanish empire.

Three centuries after colonization, Cuba remained an overlooked stopping point for Spain's fleet, which visited the Americas and returned to Spain with continental America's mineral wealth. During the 19th century, Cuba dramatically experienced a resurgence.

Haiti's collapse as a sugar-producing colony, the United States' rise as an independent nation, the ingenuity of the Creole business community of Cuba, and Spanish protective policies all led to the rise of a sugar revolution in Cuba. In a few years, Cuba became the world's major producer of sugar.

Slaves arrived in droves; sugar replaced agriculture, tobacco, and cattle as the primary economic source; large estates competed with smaller estates; Spain gave more attention to the Cuban economy; and prosperity replaced poverty. The last two factors helped in delaying a motion for independence early in the 19th century. Cuba remained loyal to Spain, as most other Latin American countries were cutting ties.

By the end of the 19th century, the loyalty of Cuba started to change as a result of Spaniards competing with Creoles for the island's governance. It led to the rise of Cuban nationalism and increased Spanish taxation and despotism. Such developments resulted in a war – The Ten Years' War – that still failed to gain independence for Cuba.

During the second independence war (1895 to 1898), José Marti – a major Cuban independence leader – was killed in battle. As a result of increasingly strained relations between the United States and Spain, the Americans entered the Cuban conflict in 1898.

Chapter 2: The Wars for Independence

As early as 1790, the idea for Cuban independence from Spain floated among some groups. José Antonio Aponte led the first revolutionary attempt in 1791. However, the uprising failed. While no uprisings occurred in the next few decades, the freedom ideal was not forgotten.

In 1825, Simón Bolivar heard of plans to liberate Cuba from Spain from a junta established in Mexico. Bolivar spoke of campaigning for Cuban independence, but the project was aborted as it was too complicated. The next serious attempt for independence occurred in 1850. Narcisó Lopez arrived from New York to Cuba with 600 men. While they conquered Cárdenas, the revolutionaries did not get popular support and they were forced to leave the island.

The next few years witnessed a few more failed attempts at independence. Beginning in 1855, conspirators were executed followed by a period of calm for over 10 years.

Cuban representatives, in 1866, traveled to Spain to meet with Spanish representatives in Madrid. The Cubans needed more investments to modernize sugar plants. The conversations failed, however, which prompted the Spaniards to lower customs rights. The Spaniards then learned that, for Cubans, the lowering of rights led to revolution and the wars for Cuban independence.

The Ten Years War

Also known as the Great War (1868 to 1878), the Ten Years War began on October 10, 1868 under Carlos Manuel de Céspedes. He was supported by the Sugar Mill La Demajagua patriots, and called for Cuba's independence. On October 11, 1868, Céspedes unsuccessfully attacked the village of Yara.

The Yara revolution extended throughout the entire area of Oriente of Cuba, and patriots converged in various parts of the island to support Céspedes. On February 27, 1874, Céspedes was killed in an ambush by Spanish troops. Activity in the Ten Years War came to a head in 1872 and 1873. However, military operations were limited to the regions of Oriente of Cuba and Camagüey due to a supplies shortage.

On February 8, 1878, peace negotiations started in Zanjón, Puerto Principe. Two days later, the governments of Spain and Cuba accepted the peace terms, and the Ten Years War ended, although protests by a group of Antonio Maceo followers continued. On May 28, 1878, Maceo ended the protests.

Smallest War

The Smallest War occurred from 1879 to 1880. On August 24, 1879, a new war against the Spanish authorities began in Oriente of Cuba. The war started because of the dissatisfaction of the revolutionaries during the Ten Years War, and the economic and political consequences of the previous war.

The new generals in the Smallest War included Calixto Garcia, Guillermo Moncada, José Maceo (Antonio's brother), Emilio Nuñez, and Francisco Carrillo. While the war was started enthusiastically, it did not gain enough magnitude as the rest of the country sought peace.

While the Smallest War lasted for less than a year, it indicated that the peace deals in Zanjón were not meant to last.

Independence War

The second war for independence occurred from 1895 to 1898. Unlike in the Ten Years War, the United States did not ignore the Cuban Independence Movement of the 1890s. The United States had become a different nation than it had been during 1865. Immigration to the United States was high, the Civil War was over, and people began to settle in the American West. Historian Stephen Ambrose had said the U.S. needed to "find a new outlet for its dynamic nature and energy."

Journalists like Joseph Pulitzer and William Randolph Hearst were fascinated with the Cuban struggle, and they used sensationalist, dramatic stories to sell their newspapers. Hearst and other journalists had succeeded to bring American attention to the Cuban people's suffering.

The 1895 revolution's central leaders included Calixto Garcia, Maximo Lopez, and Jose Marti. Gomez, who lived from 1836 to 1905, became the Cuban revolution's military leader. Garcia was instrumental to the U.S. military's success in Cuba. He provided vital intelligence to the U.S. military, including information on Spanish officers and maps. After his death, Marti became a revolutionary martyr.

Spain sent 100,000 soldiers to Cuba in 1895. After the U.S. intervened in 1898, Spanish rule in Cuba ended. However, Spain's defeat and the presence of the Americans in Cuba raised new issues for the island nation.

The Cruiser "Maine" Incident and the End of the War

President William McKinley, on January 24, 1898, deployed the USS Maine to Havana. On February 15, 1898, at 9:40 p.m., an accident (freak or sabotage) caused an explosion that killed 260 sailors and plunged the USS Maine to the ocean floor. The USS Maine was one of the U.S. Navy's new steam-powered, steel-hulled battleships, and was one of the largest battleships.

Three days after the explosion of the Maine, Hearst's newspaper sold over one million copies, becoming the first newspaper to do so. Hearst and Pulitzer's war slogan 'Remember the Maine' prompted the U.S. to intervene in the war.

On April 19, 1898, the United States Congress adopted the Joint Resolution for War with Spain, and, on April 25, 1898, the U.S. formally declared war. The would-be U.S. president, Teddy Roosevelt, resigned from his post at the Navy and joined the war. He financed personally his expedition and outfitted his 'Rough Riders' troops. The Rough Riders took the San Juan Hill away from the Spaniards.

The battle between the U.S. and Spanish naval forces – the Battle of Santiago Bay – ended centuries of Spanish conquest in the West. One American died, while 1,800

Spaniards perished in battle. The Spanish ships were either sinking, burning, or beached. The Spanish forces in Santiago surrendered two weeks later.

On August 11, 1898, the U.S. and Spain agreed on peace terms, in which the U.S. received four new territories: Puerto Rico, Cuba, Guam, and the Philippines. Spain was paid $20 million for Puerto Rico, the Philippines, and Guam.

Albeit the treaty recognized Cuban independence, the American (not the Cuban) flag was raised over Havana. During the Santiago de Cuba surrender ceremonies, Calixto Garcia and his fellow revolutionaries were not permitted to participate.

Chapter 3: U.S. Occupation and the Platt Amendment

After the Cuban war for independence, an American military government was proclaimed immediately in the island, with the installation of General John R. Brooke as commander. The Cuban revolutionary government was not allowed to take control.

General Brooke, on January 1, 1899, formally wrested control of Havana from the governor general. General Máximo Gómez, in a diary entry dated January 8, 1899, stated that "Cuba cannot have true moral peace, which is what people need for their good fortune and happiness...The transitional government was imposed by a foreign power by force and is illegitimate and incompatible with the principles that the country has been upholding..."

The U.S. government was backed by the Teller Amendment, which placed Cuba in a position different from previous Spanish colonies. The Brooke administration restored certain services while controlling postal services, customs, health agencies, and sanitation.

Brooke's successor, General Leonard Wood, in December 1899, started the second period of U.S. administration in Cuba. The progressive Wood led the most advanced Cuban reconstruction programs. He campaigned for the eradication of yellow fever and malaria in Cuba. Under Wood's administration, students were enrolled, schools were built, teachers were given special training, and the University of

Havana was rebuilt. Programs were also instituted for bridge, road, and railroad improvement.

In 1900, a new law was passed that allowed Cubans to elect leaders at a municipal level. A constitution was drafted, with a provision for universal suffrage, a bicameral legislature, an elected president, and a separation of church and state. The U.S. accepted the Cuban constitution as long as it would keep its upper hand in its dealings with Cuba. The additional clauses became known as the Platt Amendment.

The clauses stipulated that Cuba should not contract debts that may not be repaid by conventional revenues and that Cuba should not participate in treaties that may impair sovereignty. Moreover, Cuba should accept the legality of military government acts, allow the U.S. to buy or lease lands for naval stations or coaling, and give the U.S. privileges to intervene in the preservation of Cuban independence or to support a government that can protect individual liberties, life, and property.

The amendment seemed to restrict Cuban self-determination. While the Cuban assembly revised the amendment's terms, the U.S. turned it down. Due to the humiliation to the Cubans brought on by the amendment, debates ensued until the Platt Amendment was repealed in 1934.

Cuba, on June 12, 1901, ratified the amendment as an addendum to the 1901 Cuban constitution and the sole alternative to the U.S.'s permanent military occupation. The U.S., nevertheless, leased a naval coaling station at Guantanamo Bay until the 1980s. The rights were acquired under the May 1903 Treaty of Relations terms and the July 1903 Lease of Agreement. Even until today, the Guantanamo Bay issue remains a sore spot for many Cubans.

On May 20, 1902, the Cuban flag was raised over Havana as the country swore in its first president – Tomás Estrada Palma.

Chapter 4: Cuba's Reform Movements

Reformism in Cuba had begun even during the Spanish period. As the possibility of independence from Spain was still remote, several Cubans attempted to make reforms within the Spanish Empire. Reformismo (reformism) was a Cuban movement beginning in the 19th century that sought to reform Spanish institutions in Cuba.

Reformismo spurred in the middle of the century, partially because of the failure of numerous conspiracies aimed at expelling Spain and due to black uprisings against slavery in Cuba. At the time, Spain also seemed to adhere to a more lenient policy toward its Caribbean colony.

The 1865 reform movement was strong enough to organize the Partido Reformista (Reformist Party), the first political party to be established on the island. The party generally advocated for equal rights among Peninsulars and Cubans, limitation of the captain-general's powers, and greater political freedom in Cuba.

The reform party also advocated the gradual abolition of slavery, freer trade, and an increase of white migrants into the island. In 1865, the slave trade was partially abolished. On November 5, 1879, the Spanish governor signed a law abolishing slavery in Cuba. However, the royal decree that abolished slavery completely was enforced on October 7, 1886.

Some Peninsulars, who formed the Partido Incondicional Espanol (Unconditional Spanish Party), soon opposed the Reformists' activities. The Peninsulars used the Diario de la Marina newspaper to attack the Cuban reformers.

The reformists' work and their dispute with the Peninsulars affected Spain. After a successful independence movement in Santo Domingo against Spain in 1865, and at the time when Spain was experiencing political and economic difficulties, Spain's monarchy felt it was best to temper its Cuban policy.

The Junta de Informacion (Information Board) was soon established, and comprised of four Peninsulars and 12 Creole reformers. The Spanish government also ordered the Cuban municipalities to set high voting qualifications. As 12 Creoles were elected, it meant the Cubans were more open to reform than independence.

However, reforms within Cuba under Spain were short-lived. The Spanish government, while allowing the junta to meet, did not allow the implementation of the board's recommendations. In 1867, not only did the Spanish government disband the board, it also slapped on new taxes. The disbandment of the Junta de Informacion and of reformism gave rise to the independence movement. Creoles soon started to move for separation from Spain.

Agrarian Reforms

Cuba's agrarian reform laws sought to break up larger landholdings and give the back the lands to tenants, the state, and cooperatives. The land reform laws were first passed from 1959 to 1963, after the Cuban Revolution. The Argentinian revolutionary Che Guevara was declared the INRA's (Instituto Nacional de Reforma Agraria) minister of industries and oversaw the policies related to land reform.

Che Guevara, on January 27, 1959, declared that the Cuban government's main concern was 'the social justice that land redistribution brings about.' The Agrarian Reform Law went into effect on May 17, 1959. The law called for the limitation of farm sizes to 12 square kilometers (3,333 acres) and real estate to 4 square kilometers (1,000 acres).

Any holdings beyond the limits set by the law were taken by the government and were either held as state-run communities or redistributed to peasants in 271,139 square meters (67 acres). Foreigners may also not own sugar plantations.

For lands acquired by the government, the compensation was Cuban currency bonds to mature at 4.5% interest in 20 years. Bonds were based on assessed land values for tax purposes. American landowners during Fulgencio Batista's rule had lands assessed at low rates.

INRA had its own militia with 100,000 personnel. They were enlisted to help the government take control of the land and supervise distribution. The militia were later enlisted to help establish cooperative farms. U.S. corporations had owned most of the seized lands with a total area of 1,942 square kilometers (480,000 acres).

Che Guevara eventually trained the militia as a regular army. The INRA also funded most of the country's highway construction, and built tourist resorts and rural housing based on Guevara's industrial plans.

On October 1963, a Second Agrarian Reform Law was passed and enacted.

Chapter 5: The Cuban Republic and Revolution

President Tomás Estrada Palma's government was heavily influenced by the U.S. During the 1905 and 1906 elections, he tried to hold on to power. However, the Liberals contested the elections, which led to a rebellion and another United States occupation in September 1906.

William Howard Taft, the U.S. Secretary of War, attempted to resolve the issue but failed, and Palma eventually resigned. Charles Magoon was then appointed the provisional governor. In January 1909, Magoon handed the government over to José Miguel Gómez, the Liberal president. At the same time, Cuba steadily grew economically, and sugar prices continually rose until the 1920s.

However, Gómez's administration, which ran from 1909 to 1913, established a pattern of corruption, graft, fiscal irresponsibility, maladministration, and social insensitivity – particularly toward African-Cubans. Led by Pedro Ivonet and Evaristo Estenoz, the Afro-Cubans organized to secure more political patronage and better jobs.

Corruption continued under the administrations of Mario García Menocal (from 1913 to 1921), Alfredo Zayas (from 1921 to 1925), Gerardo Machado y Morales (from 1925 to 1933), Fulgencio Batista (from 1939 to 1944 and 1952 to 1959), Ramón Grau San Martin (from 1944 to 1048), and Carlos Prío Socarrás (from 1948 to 1952).

Machado was one of Cuba's most notorious presidents, holding on to power through assassinations, troops, and manipulation. In the Revolution of 1933, the U.S. government aided leftists to take Machado down. Batista then replaced Machado.

During the time, sugar comprised about 4/5 of the country's export earnings, and was supported by a tourist trade based on Havana's casinos, hotels, and brothels, especially during the United States' Prohibition years (1919 to 1933). As the 1950s ended, Cuba was one of Latin America's leading economies. However, rural workers earned only ¼ of the average $353 per capita annual income.

Most Cubans, especially those in the countryside, experienced poverty, unemployment, underemployment, and a lack of public services. The U.S. and other foreign investors had control of the economy, and Batista absolutely controlled the political system.

The Revolution and the Fall of Batista

The fall of Fulgencio Batista resulted from the country's internal political decay and Fidel Castro's 26th of July Movement, which remembered Castro's botched attack on the Moncada military base on July 26, 1953. Batista's fall may also have been due to opposition groups like Federation of University Students not satisfied with Batista's rule.

Castro, who was born on August 13, 1926, was a legislative candidate for the 1952 elections, which Batista aborted. Castro and a few of his friends, in 1955, departed for Mexico to prepare for the ousting of the

Cuban government. In December 1956, Castro and a group of rebels, were on board the yacht, Granma. Castro and his group landed in southeastern Cuba, where security forces routed and annihilated them.

Castro, his brother Raul, Che Guevara, and a few more survivors, fled to the Sierra Maestra and started a guerrilla campaign. In the following years, the rebel group had successfully recruited hundreds of Cuban volunteers. They also won battles against Batista's armed forces, and went to the island's west.

At the same time, communist groups and certain members of the non-communist Federation of University Students staged attacks and strikes in urban areas. The U.S., in 1958, cut off the Batista government with an arms embargo. Moreover, some military commanders of Cuba joined in or sympathized with the rebellion. Early on January 1, 1959, Batista fled the country. After he departed, around 800 Castro supporters set into Havana, having overcome a 30,000-strong army.

The Aftermath

The 26th of July Movement had relatively insignificant support, vague political plans, and untested governing skills. However, the movement rapidly forged a following among urban workers, poor peasants, idealists, and the youth. Dating to 1925, the Communist Party of Cuba assumed the country's main political role. The country then patterned itself on Eastern Europe's Soviet-bloc countries, and Cuba became the Americas' first socialist country.

Castro's new regime effectively dissolved Cuba's capitalist system by collectivizing agricultural production, setting up a centrally-planned economy, forging close economic ties with the Soviet Union, and developing various social services – especially in the rural areas.

The new regime also eradicated what's left of Batista's army and established new institutions of farmers and professional workers. The Castro regime nationalized hundreds of millions of dollars in private businesses and U.S. property. Such acts by the new regime set off the U.S. government's retaliatory measures like a trade embargo and an invasion (unsuccessful) by Cuban exiles at the Bay of Pigs in April 1961. More operations to overthrow Castro did not succeed and he went on to become one of the world's longest-ruling presidents. Batista died on August 6, 1973 in Estoril, Portugal at the age of 72.

Chapter 6: The Castro Era

The United States' antagonistic actions, however, only pushed Fidel Castro to the Soviet Union and strengthened popular support for him. In December of 1961, Castro declared that he was a communist.

The Cuban leadership and the country in general were divided over Cuba's shift to communism and the country's increasing dependence on the Soviet Union. Hundreds of thousands of Cuban investors and skilled workers defected to the United States (mainly to Miami, Florida) and other countries like Spain.

In the initial years of Fidel Castro's administration, Soviet military and economic support were crucial, and the Soviets' moves often roused strong opposition from the United States.

The October 1962 Cuban Missile Crisis was a serious incident. After the Union of Soviet Socialist Republics (U.S.S.R.) installed nuclear missile stations on the island, the world was almost at war, and the United States installed a naval blockade of Cuba and demanded the Soviets to remove the missiles.

The island country was also affected by shortages of fuel, food, and other necessities. The second agrarian reform law in 1963 ended the diversification attempts on the economy, which was still dependent of sugar cane. In 1964, Cuba renewed efforts to export revolution by meeting with Latin American communists in Havana. In 1965, Cuba almost stoked a civil war in the Dominican Republic, which prompted the United States military to intervene in Cuba's neighbor.

In Kinshasa, Congo, Che Guevara engaged in covert operations. In 1967, Guevara was killed while trying to start a revolution in Bolivia. Afterwards, many Caribbean states and Latin American countries alienated Cuba for its attempts to brew conflict.

In the late 1960s, the Cuban government restored its attacks on private property by nationalizing numerous small businesses. Officers of the military occupied high posts in industry, the government, and the Cuban Communist Party. Castro's regime sought to foster nationalism and boost production by offering moral incentives and encouraging labor organizations.

The Castro government eventually returned to Soviet-style planning and a conventional system of socialist incentives. A new constitution in 1976 and a new code for elections reorganized the country's political system. Fidel Castro became president of the Council of State and of the Council of Ministers; thus, combining effectively the roles of prime minister and president.

During the 1970s, conditions improved. Shortages and bottlenecks were significantly eliminated. Isolation from world diplomacy gained Cuba a leadership role among non-aligned nations and developing countries. Cubans offered commercial, military, and technical assistance to several states in Latin America, Africa, and the Caribbean region. Cuba, however, lost influence as it supported the 1979 Soviet invasion of Afghanistan.

In the 1980s, Cuban military assistance influenced civil wars in Ethiopia and Angola, and civilian personnel contributed to Latin America and Asia. In 1983, the U.S. invaded Grenada, killing dozens of Cubans and banishing from the island what was left of Cuba's aid force. From 1989 to 1991, Cuba slowly removed its troops from Angola.

Soviet aid to Cuba in the forms of war material, petroleum, loans, and technical advice was vital and comprised a major portion of the country's annual budget. The U.S.S.R. also bought a significant portion of Cuban sugar at generally higher prices.

Soviet-Cuban relations crumbled as Soviet economic, social, and political policies were liberalized during the late 1980s. However, the Cuban government did not modify its stance on economic and social policy.

In September 1991, Soviet troops started to withdraw its troops from Cuba over the island country's objections that withdrawing troops would compromise Cuba's security. Cuba's troubled economy, when the U.S.S.R. dissolved later in 1991, further suffered from the loss of vital economic and military support that had effectively constituted subsidies.

In the middle of internal shortages, and with dissatisfaction and unrest growing, Fidel Castro announced a 'special period in peacetime' of energy conservation, reduced public services, and food rationing. Aside from the increase in unemployment, the ongoing trade embargo by the U.S. worsened shortages of medical supplies, food shortages, fuel, and raw materials.

The government, in 1993, legalized small businesses like family restaurants (paladres), U.S. dollar use, and private employment. In 1994, independent farmers' markets and farms were encouraged. The Cuban government also attracted non-Cuban capitalists, including Spanish and Canadian hoteliers.

In 1997, Christmas again became a national holiday, in anticipation of Pope John Paul II's visit in 1998. Led by tourism, Cuba's economy significantly improved. However, Cubans were starting to doubt socialism's future.

After Cuba downed two U.S. aircraft in 1996, the U.S. Congress passed the Helms-Burton Law, which threatened to sanction foreign companies investing in Cuba. Dissidents in Cuba, in 1999, were jailed. Early in the 21st century, Cuba gained from a Venezuelan petroleum trade agreement, which eased some of Cuba's more restrictive social and economic policies.

Fidel Castro, on July 31, 2006, provisionally passed on power to his brother, Raul Castro, as the former recovered from intestinal surgery. Fidel Castro, in February 2008, stated officially that he would not accept another presidential term. The Cuban National Assembly then chose Raul as the country's next leader.

Under Raul, Cuba implemented several reforms. The country's equal pay system was abolished. Cubans are now allowed to buy personal computers and cellular phones, and can stay at hotels reserved formerly for foreigners.

In 2003, the European Union sanctioned Cuba for repression of its dissidents. The European Union lifted the sanctions in 2008, prompting criticism from the United States. In September 2010, Raul Castro announced the toleration of private enterprises and laid off around 500,000 government employees.

The National Assembly, in 2011, approved measures to free up the economy. Some of the steps include the state's reduced role in the retail, transportation, construction, and agricultural sectors, along with the encouragement of private business development.

By 2012, some estimated 390,000 Cubans had started cuenta-propistas (self-employment enterprises) including businesses like auto-repair shops, beauty parlors, restaurants, and taxi services. On February 2013, Raul Castro announced that he would not seek for reelection when his term would end in 2018.

Chapter 7: Cuba in the Cold War Era

Cuba has significantly figured in the Cold War with the Bay of Pigs Invasion and the Cuban Missile Crisis. While Cubans welcomed Castro's overthrow of Batista, Cuba's new political order made American government officials nervous. Although considered repressive and corrupt, Batista was an ally to U.S. companies and was pro-American. Batista was anti-communist and did not restrict American operations in Cuba.

Fidel Castro, on the other hand, disapproved of how Americans conducted business in Cuba. He believed it was time for Cubans to take control of their nation. One of his popular slogans was "Cuba Sí, Yanquis No."

Upon assuming power, Castro moved to reduce American influence on Cuba. He nationalized American-controlled industries like mining and sugar, called on fellow Latin American governments to be more autonomous, and announced land reform plans.

As a response, U.S. President Dwight D. Eisenhower authorized the Central Intelligence Agency (CIA) to recruit 1,400 Miami-based Cuban exiles and train them to overthrow Castro.

Castro, in May 1960, established ties with the Soviet Union, and the U.S. retaliated by banning Cuban sugar importation. To prevent the collapse of the sugar economy, the Soviet Union agreed to purchase the sugar. The U.S. government, in January 1961, cut diplomatic ties with Cuba and began preparations for an invasion.

Several State Department and other advisors to John F. Kennedy, the new American president, asserted that Castro would not be an American threat. However, Kennedy believed that orchestrating Castro's removal would show China, Russia, and skeptical Americans that he was determined to win the Cold War.

President Kennedy had inherited his predecessor's campaign to equip and train a Cuban exile guerrilla army, but he had doubts about the plan's wisdom. Officers of the CIA informed Kennedy they could keep a covert involvement in the invasion. If all goes well, the plan would spur an anti-Castro uprising on Cuba.

The plan's first part was to destroy Castro's air force. A group of Cuban exiles, on April 15, 1961 departed Nicaragua in American B-26 bombers, painted to resemble stolen Cuban planes. The exiles struck the Cuban airfields. However, Castro knew of the plan and moved his planes to a safe location.

The Cuban exile brigade, on April 17, 1961, started its invasion at an area on Cuba's southern shore – the Bay of Pigs. However, the invasion was unsuccessful. While the CIA sought secrecy on the operation, a radio station had broadcast every detail of the operation all over Cuba. Furthermore, backup paratroopers set foot in the wrong area.

Not long after, Castro's troops caught the beach invaders, and the exiles surrendered in less than one day. Over 1,100 were taken prisoner and 114 were killed. Another diplomatic misfire, the 1962 Cuban missile crisis, further fanned American-Cuban-Soviet tensions.

The Cuban Missile Crisis

On October 1962, leaders of the United States and the Soviet Union, during the Cuban Missile Crisis, engaged in a 13-day military and political standoff over the installation of Soviet missiles (nuclear-armed) in Cuba.

In an October 22, 1962 television address, President Kennedy informed the Americans about the missiles' presence, explained why he enacted a naval blockade surrounding Cuba, and made clear the U.S. was ready to forcefully neutralize the national security threat.

A crucial Cuban missile crisis event occurred on October 24, 1962, when Cuba-bound Soviet ships approached the group of U.S. vessels enforcing the blockade. A Soviet attempt to breach the blockade could have likely sparked a confrontation and an eventual nuclear exchange. However, the Soviets did not breach the blockade.

The standoff between the U.S. and the Soviet Union continued. On October 27, 1962, an American reconnaissance plane was brought down over the island, and an invasion force was being prepared in Florida.

While many people on both sides feared the crisis would have led to World War III, the American and Soviet leaders found a way out of the situation. Meanwhile, the Soviets and Americans had communicated with one another. On October 26, 1962, Khrushchev informed Kennedy, offering to remove missiles from Cuba in exchange for a promise from American leaders not to invade Cuba.

The next day, Khrushchev proposed to the U.S. that the U.S.S.R. would take away its missiles in Cuba if the

Americans removed their Turkey missile installations. The Kennedy administration officially decided to comply with the first message's terms and ignore entirely Khrushchev's second letter. In private, however, the U.S. agreed to withdraw the U.S. missiles in Turkey.

Robert Kennedy, the U.S. attorney general at the time, delivered in person the message to the Soviet ambassador in Washington. On October 28, 1962, the Cuban Missile Crisis ended.

The Cuban Missile Crisis had a sobering effect on both the Soviets and Americans. In 1963, a direct communication link was established between Moscow and Washington to help defuse further diplomatic situations, and the two world powers signed treaties related to nuclear artillery.

Chapter 8: Cuba-U.S. Relations and the Trade Embargo

The relationship of Cuba and the United States began when the latter started to intervene in Cuba's wars for independence against Spain. While the U.S. helped Cuba achieve independence, and even briefly colonized Cuba until 1902, the military of the U.S. continued to intervene in Cuba's affairs until 1934. The U.S. also continued to dominate trade within Cuba until 1953.

Below are some of the highlights of Cuban relations with the United States.

In 1953, Fidel Castro, who was a lawyer, led the revolution against Fulgencio Batista. The U.S. sold arms to Batista, who was their ally, even if he resisted calls to step down or reform. Around 1958, Batista began to be defeated by Castro. The U.S. subsequently denied asylum to Batista, who eventually settled in Portugal.

In April 1959, Castro accepted an invitation from U.S. newspapers to visit New York, where he visited the Bronx Zoo and Yankee Stadium, spoke before the Council of Foreign Affairs, and met editors. Instead of meeting U.S. President Dwight Eisenhower, Castro met Richard Nixon, U.S.'s then-vice president, and Dean Acheson, the secretary of state.

In April 1961, the botched Bay of Pigs invasion was carried out. Shortly after, on October 1962, Cuba got embroiled in the U.S.-Soviet Union conflict in a historical event that was known as the Cuban Missile Crisis.

A few decades later, on April 1980, the Mariel Boatlift event occurred. The event was a mass emigration of Cubans, who traveled from Cuba to the U.S. between April 15, 1980 and October 31, 1980. Due to decades of economic sluggishness in Cuba, numerous Cubans swarmed Havana's Peruvian embassy after an escape attempt there left the compound unprotected.

Castro gave in to pressure and opened the doors for migration to the United States. However, he wavered on transport. The Cuban exiles in Florida amassed a fleet of 1,700 boats. By May 1980, over 100,000 Cubans landed on Florida, in which the activity overwhelmed the U.S. coast guard. Eventually, the Castro regime and U.S. President Jimmy Carter agreed mutually to end the exodus.

In November 2001, there was a slight break in the United States' trade embargo against Cuba. After Hurricane Michelle, four American food companies, including Riceland Foods and Cargill, were allowed to sell food to Cuba. Castro did not accept the offer of Washington to send humanitarian aid via non-government organizations (NGOs). However, he said he was prepared, "to acquire certain quantities of medicine and food from the United States, paying them in cash."

The years from October 2003 to December 2009 were a period of tension and change. After a tension-filled decade, including the 2000 custody battle of Elian Gonzalez and the 1996 downing of two American planes by Cuba, President George W. Bush tightened the United States' sanctions on Cuba.

Recovering from intestinal surgery, Fidel Castro, in 2006, transferred power to his brother Raul Castro. Furthermore, a delegation from the U.S. comprised of

Democrats and Republicans from Congress visit Cuba; however, they were not able to meet Raul Castro.

U.S. President Barack Obama, in 2009, eased money transfers and travel for Cuban families split between the two nations. Meanwhile, Alan Gross – an American – was imprisoned and accused of spying in Cuba.

In December 2013, a handshake between Obama and Raul Castro at a memorial for Nelson Mandela offered hope for improved U.S.-Cuban relations. In December 2014, a reconciliation between the papacy and Cuba was brokered. Senior officials in Havana and Washington made tentative steps for peace. Furthermore, Pope Francis (the first Latin American pope) sent letters personally to Raul Castro and Obama, urging reconciliation.

Canada and the Vatican also hosted diplomatic meetings. Over a period of 18 months, Havana and Washington agreed to slowly thaw diplomatic relations. In December of 2014, Raul Castro and Obama stated they would normalize diplomatic relations – despite the Congress-mandated trade embargo. Moreover, Raul Castro and Obama also agreed to free Alan Gross and three Cubans for spying.

In a speech, Raul Castro emphasized the need to remove U.S. commercial, financial, and economic blockade of Cuba. The embargo, which was codified by U.S. law, was subject to the U.S. Congress's action and beyond the scope of the executive authority of President Obama.

The Embargo

When Fidel Castro assumed power in 1959, most of the Cuban economy was under the control of American corporations. The industries controlled by U.S. firms included railroads and utilities. The American firms also controlled a huge portion of Cuba's natural resources like cattle, sugar, timber, tobacco, mining, oil, and most of the nation's farmland.

Castro's government nationalized the U.S. assets, and claimed them in the name of the Cuban citizens. The U.S. then made a series of retaliatory attacks. One of them was the trade embargo, which was an effort to topple Castro's government. After over half a century, which saw the Soviet Union breakup, the Cold War's end, and the transfer of power from Fidel Castro to Raul Castro, it is apparent that the trade embargo did not succeed.

Many argue today that the embargo has no real purpose. For them, ending the embargo will make consumers in the U.S. happy. Ending it will also boost the U.S. economy and bring a certain level of economic freedom to Cuba.

Not only has the trade of U.S. goods to Cuba been halted, but also a large degree of travel and tourism. In 1960, the initial trade restrictions on Cuba were implemented under U.S. President Eisenhower's time. The U.S. placed exports to Cuba under validated license controls, with the exception of non-subsidized medicines, medical supplies, and food. However, the action did not include travel restrictions.

President Kennedy, on February 1962, imposed the trade embargo due to Cuba's ties with the Soviet Union. On July 9, 1963, the U.S. Department of the Treasury's

OFAC (Office of Foreign Assets) issued the Cuban Assets Control Regulations that banned travel by restricting any transactions with the communist island nation.

In March 1977, the Carter administration announced the lifting of travel restrictions to Cuba from the U.S., wherein such restrictions have been implemented since the 1960s. Carter issued a travel-related transaction license for Americans visiting Cuba. Also allowed were direct flights from the U.S. mainland to Cuba.

In April 1982, President Ronald Reagan's administration re-imposed Cuba travel restrictions. However, several travel categories were allowed, including travel by filmmaking or news organization employees, U.S. government officials, persons visiting close relatives, or persons doing professional research. It did not allow ordinary business or tourist travel.

On May 13, 1999, the OFAC issued changes to the embargo regulations, which loosened restrictions on travel categories, and allowing travel for people-to-people educational exchange travel. In 2000, the OFAC granted the first specific license for such kind of travel.

On March 24, 2003, travel regulations to Cuba were amended and eliminated the people-to-people exchange licenses. On April 13, 2009, U.S. President Obama directed loosened restrictions on financial remittances and family travel. Obama's administration also widened the scope of eligible donations with gift parcels. The administration also increased links to telecommunications with Cuba.

On January 14, 2011, Obama announced that changes be made to certain policies and regulations. The measures were meant to: support Cuba's civil society, increase people-to-people contact, enhance the flow of information among Cubans, and help to promote Cubans' information independence from government authorities.

On January 16, 2015, new regulations concerning travel to Cuba are drafted. Americans can now easily travel to Cuba. In 2016, commercial flights from the U.S. mainland to Cuba are offered.

Chapter 9: The History of Havana

As the capital of Cuba, the history of Havana is much more diverse and turbulent than the rest of the country. On August 25, 2015, Diego Velázquez de Cuéllar established Havana on the island's southern coast – on the Mayabeque River banks. A 1514 map of Cuba sets the town at the mouth of the Mayabeque River.

Havana's present location was established in 1519, on a site called Puerto de Carenas ('Careening Bay'). Pánfilo de Narváez gave Havana the name San Cristóbal de la Habana. Havana started as a trading port, and was regularly attacked by pirates, French corsairs, and buccaneers. The attacks prompted the Spanish Crown to fund the main cities' first fortresses.

Ships from around the New World transported products to Havana, in order for them to be taken to Spain. The multitude of ships also fueled Havana's manufacturing and agriculture. King Philip II of Spain, on December 20, 1592, declared Havana a city.

During the 17th century, Havana expanded with the construction of buildings made out of wood. Such buildings combined Canarian characteristics and Iberian architecture styles. In 1649, a third of Havana's population was struck by an epidemic from Cartagena, Colombia. By 1740, Havana had become the Spanish Empire's only New World dry dock.

The British captured Havana during the Seven Years War beginning on June 6, 1762. Upon conquering Havana, the British established trade with their Caribbean and North American colonies. Less than one year after Havana was captured, the Peace of Paris was signed; thus, ending the war. The treaty handed over Florida to Britain in exchange for returning Havana to Spain.

After Spain regained control of the city, Havana was transformed into one of the Americas' heavily-fortified cities. On January 15, 1796, Christopher Columbus's remains were brought to Cuba from Santo Domingo. His remains rested in Havana until 1898.

During the early 19th century, trade between North America and the Caribbean flourished, and Havana thrived. Prosperity among the population led to the construction of new mansions, and Havana was considered the Paris of the Antilles.

The first railroad was built in 1837 and it was used to transport sugar to the Havana harbor. Slavery was legal in Cuba until the 1880s. After the Confederates were defeated in 1865 during the Civil War, former slaveholders in the U.S. moved to Havana and continued their operations. The city's walls were dismantled in 1863 to pave way for the metropolis's expansion.

After the War for Independence

Like in the rest of Cuba, Havana was also occupied by the United States during the turn of the 20th century. The occupation ended officially on May 20, 1902, when Tomás Estrada Palma took office as Cuba's first president.

During the Republican Period, which lasted from 1902 to 1959, Havana and the rest of Cuba experienced a boost in the economy. During the 1930s, casinos, luxury hotels, and nightclubs were built to serve the city's growing tourism industry. During the time, Havana also hosted numerous activities like musical shows, parks, Grand Prix car racing, and marinas. Around 300,000 Americans visited Havana in 1958.

After the 1959 revolution, Castro's new regime promised to improve public housing, official buildings, and social services. From May of 1959 onwards, Castro appropriated all private industry and property under a communist model supported by the Soviet Union after the trade embargo by the United States. Havana was especially hit hard by the shortages.

After the Soviet Union's decline in 1991, the Soviet subsidies stopped. Despite the political upheavals in Europe after the fall of the Soviet Union and the emergence of new countries, Havana still continued to have a communist government throughout the 1990s.

Havana is currently being renovated. After decades of prohibition, the government turned to tourism for a new revenue stream. Foreign investors are now allowed to develop the hospitality industry and construct new hotels. Old Havana has also undergone rehabilitation, with the revitalization of public squares and streets. However, revitalization efforts are concentrated in less than 10% of Old Havana's land area due to the city's large size.

Conclusion

The death of Fidel Castro on November 25, 2016 ushered in a new era for Cuba. However, change had begun when the older Castro – due to a serious illness in 2006 – handed power in 2008 to his younger brother, Raul.

Under his rule, Raul Castro moved to adjust Cuba's state-controlled system that was meant to salvage the Cuban Revolution's gains while veering its economy away from heavy reliance on Chinese largesse and Venezuelan subsidies. Under Raul, Cuba accepted new foreign investment and recovered diplomacy with the United States.

The U.S.-Cuba normalization process, which culminated in U.S. President Barack Obama's March 2016 visit, has promoted better ties to benefit both countries. However, Raul's Cuban socialism 'updating' has been limited, due in part to Fidel's shadow and his followers and their opposition to Washington, the U.S. embargo, and the Cuban exiles in Miami.

The U.S. has affected Cuba in many ways, and imperialists throughout Cuba's history have negatively and positively changed the country. Cuba is country with a brutal past and a shaky present.

Despite the country's economic and political situation, the Cuban culture still is a draw for many a tourist. As the country's main income stream, tourism is also being updated to offer more to local and foreign visitors. Cuba's future is bright, though, as the country is opening up its doors to other countries once again.

Printed in Great Britain
by Amazon